To my mother, Gerri, for her endless love

JANETTA OTTER-BARRY BOOKS

Eye on the Wild: Lion copyright © Frances Lincoln Limited 2012
Text and photographs copyright © Suzi Eszterhas 2012

The right of Suzi Eszterhas to be identified as the author and photographer of this work
has been asserted by her in accordance with the Copyright, Designs and Patents Act,
1988 (United Kingdom).]

First published in Great Britain and in the USA in 2012
Frances Lincoln Children's Books, 4 Torriano Mews,
Torriano Avenue, London NW5 2RZ
www.franceslincoln.com

This paperback edition first published in Great Britain in 2012

A catalogue record for this book is available from the British Library.

ISBN 978-1-84780-311-5

Set in Stempel Schneidler

Printed in China

1 3 5 7 9 8 6 4 2

LION

Suzi Eszterhas

F

FRANCES LINCOLN
CHILDREN'S BOOKS

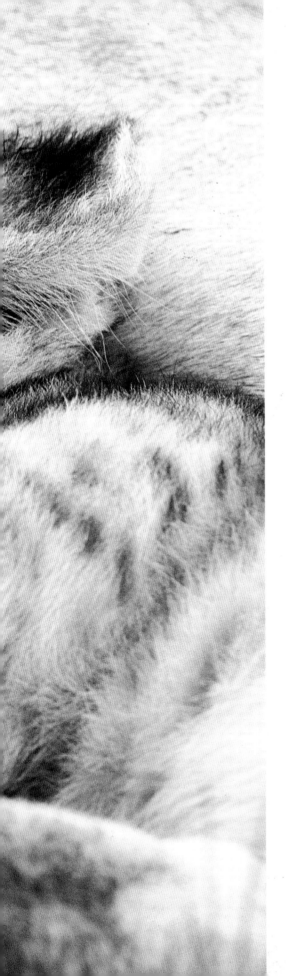

In a grassy den, on the African savannah, a newborn lion snuggles up to her mum. The little baby is called a cub. She is born with her eyes and ears closed, and can barely crawl, so she spends the first two months of her life here, safely tucked up with her sister.

When she is two weeks old, the cub's eyes and ears have opened. Her furry coat is brown and covered with small spots, which help to keep her hidden in the grass. She is still tiny and wobbly on her feet and spends all her time cuddled up next to Mum.

In the safety of the den, the cub starts to grow bigger. She spends a lot of time playing with her sister. They pounce on each other, play hide-and-seek, climb bushes, and chew on twigs. Mum is always fun to play with, too. Chewing her tail is one of their favourite games.

Mum is careful to keep her cubs well hidden. Sometimes she moves them to a new place so that male lions, hyenas and other dangerous animals can't find them. The cub is still too small and wobbly to walk far, so Mum carries her in her mouth. But she is very gentle and makes sure her sharp teeth don't hurt.

The growing cub is always hungry and she drinks Mum's milk all day long. The milk tastes good and will help her to grow big and strong. In years to come, she will grow up to be one of the largest cats in the world.

After two months of living in the den, Mum takes her cubs to meet the rest of their lion family, or 'pride'. The little cub meets her aunts, cousins and older brothers and sisters for the first time. Many lion mothers have babies at the same time, so lots of the cub's cousins are the same age. Now she has some other little lions to play with.

It's also time for the cub to meet her father, the king of the pride. He's huge – nearly twice as big as her mother – so she's a little bit shy at first. But, with Mum standing close by, she is finally brave enough to say hello. Dad is friendly and nuzzles her gently.

Dad has long golden hair around his head. This is called a mane. He is the toughest lion and has a very important job, protecting the pride and its home from strangers. He is always busy keeping a look-out for enemies.

Lion school begins very early and the three-month-old cub and her sister have a lot to learn. Mum takes them out on to the open plains to explore their world for the first time. The cub has many adventures. She climbs little mountains, crosses muddy streams, hisses at raindrops when they fall on puddles, and even finds a ball of elephant poo to play with.

Sometimes, after a day of adventure and exploring, the cub gets dirty. Like all good lion mothers, Mum is careful to keep her cub clean. Her tongue is rough like sandpaper and she uses it to scrub every bit of dirt off her baby. The cub loves to be groomed and sits there patiently until she is dirt-free.

Soon, everyone is hungry and it's time for Mum to go hunting. She leaves the cubs behind, safely tucked away under a bush, and heads out into the long grass to look for zebras, antelopes, buffaloes and other animals to hunt. She will use her keen eyesight, good hearing and strong sense of smell to find her food.

When she is six months old, the cub stops drinking Mum's milk and eats meat instead. She eats whatever animals Mum catches and seems to enjoy feasting on the delicious meat. Somehow, she knows that it might be a few days before they can eat again, so she gobbles up as much as she can, as fast as she can.

After filling her tummy with meat, the cub likes to take a nap in the shade. She stays cool by lying on her back or side with her big belly in the air. Sleeping is one of the cub's favourite things to do. Even adult lions like to sleep for most of the day.

On her first birthday
the cub is ready to learn
the most important lesson
of all – how to catch food.
This can be difficult, so the
family works together as
a team. It's exciting – and
scary – to be taken out
on to the plains with some
of the other cubs, to learn
how to hunt.

Learning how to hunt takes
a long time. Lions hide in long grass
and sneak up on the animals they
are trying to catch. But sometimes
the young cub is clumsy and the
prey animals spot her and run away.
The cub keeps trying and, with
the help of her family, she slowly
gets better and better. Eventually,
she will become a great hunter.

After two years, the young lion has grown up. She has learned how to hunt for food, keep herself clean and healthy, and stay away from danger. Her mum and aunts have also taught her how to be a good mother, and soon she'll bring cubs of her own into the pride. But she will never leave home – she will remain with her pride for the rest of her life.

More about Lions

- The lion is often called the 'King of the Jungle' but lions don't live in the jungle. Instead, they live in the grassy areas of Africa and the forests of north-west India.

- A male lion can weigh up to 225 kilograms or 500 pounds – that's heavier than about 60 house cats combined – and is the second-largest cat in the world, after the tiger.

- The lion is the only social cat in the world and lives in families, or prides, of up to 40 individuals.

- Lions have incredible eyesight and can see five times better than humans.

- Hunting is hard work for lions – only 1 in 4 hunts is successful.

- Male lions with the biggest and darkest manes are more likely to be the healthiest and most aggressive.

- A male lion can eat nearly 45 kilograms or 100 pounds of meat in one day. That's like eating about 400 hamburgers.

- The lion is an endangered species, because it is hunted in many parts of Africa and people are destroying its home.

- For more information visit www.bornfree.org.uk

Collect all the books in the EYE ON THE WILD series –
a brilliant introduction to animals in the wild,
from birth to adulthood

Cheetah
ISBN 978-1-84780-307-8

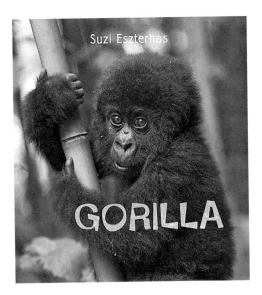

Gorilla
ISBN 978-1-84780-305-4

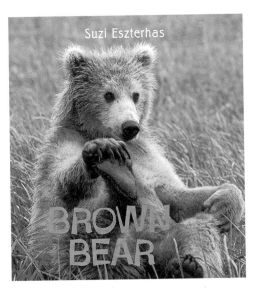

Brown Bear
ISBN 978-1-84780-308-5

Lion
ISBN 978-1-84780-311-5

Frances Lincoln titles are available from all good bookshops.
You can also buy books and find out more about your favourite titles,
authors and illustrators on our website: www.franceslincoln.com